THE CHILL
of MARBLE

THE CHILL
of MARBLE

A COMMONPLACE
COLLECTION *by*

GEORGE HERRICK

THE IPSWICH PRESS
IPSWICH, MASSACHUSETTS

ACKNOWLEDGMENTS

The editor gratefully acknowledges his indebtedness to the following publishers and copyright proprietors for the use of selections from the works indicated below:

From *The Autobiography of Johann Wolfgang von Goethe.* Copyright © 1949 by Public Affairs Press, Washington, D.C.

From *A Chime of Words—The Letters of Logan Pearsall Smith.* Copyright © 1984 by John Russell (Ticknor & Fields, New York).

From *The Fringes of Power—10 Downing Street Diaries,* by John Colville. Copyright © 1985 by Hodder and Stoughton Ltd., London.

From *Italian Journey* by Johann Wolfgang von Goethe, translation by W. H. Auden and Elizabeth Mayer. Copyright © 1962 by Pantheon Books, a division of Random House, Inc., New York.

From *Lanterns on the Levee—Recollections of a Planter's Son* by William Alexander Percy. Copyright © 1941 by Alfred A. Knopf, Inc., New York.

From *The Letters of Gustave Flaubert, 1830-1857.* Copyright © 1979, 1980 by Francis Steegmuller (Harvard University Press, Cambridge).

From *The Long March* by Harrison Salisbury. Copyright © 1985 by Harrison Salisbury (Harper & Row, Publishers, Inc., New York).

From *Mary Berenson—A Self Portrait from Her Letters & Diaries.* Copyright © 1983 by Barbara Strachey (W.W. Norton & Company, Inc., New York).

From *North to the Orient* by Anne Morrow Lindbergh. Copyright © 1935 renewed 1963 by Anne Morrow Lindbergh (Harcourt Brace Jovanovich, Inc., Orlando).

From *The Pebbled Shore* by Elizabeth Longford. Copyright © 1986 by Elizabeth Harman Packenham, Countess of Longford (Alfred A. Knopf, Inc., New York).

From *With an Eye to the Future* by Osbert Lancaster. Copyright © 1967 by Osbert Lancaster (John Murray (Publishers) Ltd., London).

Published by
THE IPSWICH PRESS
Box 291
Ipswich, Massachusetts 01938

ISBN 0-938864-11-4

For

My sister, Nina

Contents

Preface

Recalling favorite or striking passages from our reading is a pastime familiar to all. One may collect such commonplace pieces for one's own pleasure, compile them for that of friends, or offer them for the enjoyment of a wider public. Another motive is encouraging others to do the same. There is a sense, too, of preserving what we risk forgetting.

This is a sequel to my first collection, *Michelangelo's Snowman* (1985), which promised periodic offerings as having more vitality than a comprehensive edition later in the day. So it mainly reflects enthusiasms and discoveries of the past three years. Many other passages, even perhaps more interesting ones, lie in my store of notes and jottings, which accumulates with almost every book I read or gathering I attend. But it was these choices which served to create the mood, establish the pattern and set the tone which come together here.

As a matter of personal preference I try to limit myself to books in my own library or those with which I have had some special encounter. Professional librarians—if they would share their spoils—would have different criteria. Equally, other readers would bring different antennae to the recognition of choice passages.

Here then is a second small collection. In one way or another these pieces have entertained me, added to the treasury of better known material on a given theme, or suggested a new avenue for collection.

GEORGE GARDNER HERRICK

Roque Island, Maine
15 September 1988

I. Prologue

Que d'un art délicat les pièces assorties
N'y forment qu'un seul tout de diverses parties.

Nicolas Boileau Despréaux,
Art poétique (1669-1674)

I called on Erskine and related to him the history of the opera. I was in an immoderate flow of the spirits and raged away. He gave me a very sensible advice against repeating what people said, which may do much harm. I have an unlucky custom of doing so.

James Boswell,
London Journal, 1762-1765

The diary had opened only on 15 November 1762. Luckily Boswell ignored the advice and overcame any apprehension about the task on which he was embarked. Hon. Andrew Erskine was an indolent versifier and man about town.

A delightful letter opening, to Helen Thomas Flexner:

July 21, 1905

Thy charming letter (and no one's letters have a charm like thine) has been looking at me on my desk for some time, and I have been waiting for the moment, the mood, when I could dip in something out of the wells and springs of my life, to send thee in return for the cool and pleasant taste thee gives me of thy thoughts . . .

Logan Pearsall Smith

Smith was an American Quaker man of letters, remembered for his collections of Trivia, *who spent most of his life in England. Helen Flexner was Smith's first cousin, and mother of the American historian James Thomas Flexner.*

Thus did Gibbon arm himself for his Transalpine expedition in 1764-1765 from Switzerland through Italy:

In the country, Horace and Virgil, Juvenal and Ovid, were my assiduous companions: but, in town, I formed and executed a plan of study for the use of my Transalpine expedition: the topography of old Rome, the ancient geography of Italy, and the science of medals. 1. I diligently read, almost always with a pen in my hand, the elaborate treatises of Nardini, Donatus, etc., which fill the fourth volume of the Roman Antiquities of Graevius. 2. I next undertook and finished the Italia Antiqua of Cluverius, a learned native of Prussia, who had measured, on foot, every spot, and has compiled and digested every passage of the ancient writers. These passages in Greek or Latin authors I perused in the text of Cluverius, in two folio volumes: but I separately read the descriptions of Italy by Strabo, Pliny, and Pomponius Mela, the catalogues of the epic poets, the Itineraries of Wesseling's Antonius, and the coasting voyage of Rutilius Numatianus; and I studied two kindred subjects in the Mesures Itinéraires of d'Anville, and the copious work of Bergier, Histoire des grands Chemins de l'Empire Romain. From these materials I formed a table of roads and distances reduced to our English measure; filled a folio commonplace-book with my recollections and remarks on the geography of Italy . . .

Edward Gibbon,
Memoirs (1796)

The index of The Stuffed Owl *is a delight which stands alone as entertainment:*

Gabriel, the Archangel, titivates himself, 25
Gases, goings-on of, 108
George II, his particularly nice virtues, 9; his half-share in
the universe, 52; his fortunate philoprogenitiveness, 52,
54; his blooming honours, 68; his godlike appearance,ibid.
George III unlocks chaste Beauty's adamantine zone, 93;
enters Paradise, 132
German place-names, the poet does his best with, 54
Gill, Harry, his extensive yet inadequate wardrobe, 144
Gloucester, Duke of, a heavy-weight, 31
Goats, Welsh, their agility envied by botanist, 82
Golf, a remedy for unemployment, 16
Gouge, Rev. T., brought to dust, 49
Grapes and embrocations, suitable gifts for invalids, 213
Grave, living, see Shark; rose-covered, 4, 160; suicide's,
rendezvous at a, 86; mother's, habit of dancing on,
reprobated, 218
Gravy, blood and, 16
Great Exhibition, the, its contents compendiously catalogued,
243
Guardian Angel, Miss Jewsbury's, has a pressing
engagement, 151
Gunston, Mr., admits superiority of heavenly architecture,
48

17

Hags, midnight, damned vigils of, ignored by pensive poet, 137
Handkerchiefs, relays of, called for, 16
Harp-String, damped by poet's tears, 169
Hats, unfashionable in heaven, 216
Hatter affords relief to ram, 77
Heart wins over Art every time, 13
Heaven, system of bookkeeping in, 32; vogue of Mr. Purcell's music in, 37; unexpected grandeur of its architecture, 48; knowledge of languages useful in, ibid.; blasted, 188; haloes the only wear in, 216
Henry spares no expense in his nefarious designs on Jessy, 82
Henry II, urged to get a move on, 46; his pleasing anguish, ibid.
Hinds, salubrious, 14; athletic, 60. See also Swains
Hope, a high-kicker, 1
Hops need props, 97
Horns, Conchimarian, 185
Hottentots, uncommercial parricides, 77

D. B. Wyndham Lewis and Charles Lee,
The Stuffed Owl, An Anthology of Bad Verse (1930)

II. At Play With Words

William Lyon Phelps, professor of English literature at Yale from 1892 to 1933, has left us a small collection of his favorite typographical errors.

Perhaps the most fascinating typographical error I ever heard of was described, curiously enough, by Herbert Spencer. A devout Christian woman wrote a book upholding self-sacrifice and toward its close came this sentence: *"Pour bien comprendre l'amour, il faut sortir de soi."* In the irrevocable book it appeared thus: *"Pour bien comprendre l'amour, il faut sortir le soir."*

Autobiography (1938)

Compare Rossetti's five sweet symphonies with Swinburne's less
successful attempt to achieve musicality with girls' names:

"We two," she said, "will seek the groves
    Where Lady Mary is,
With her five handmaidens, whose names
    Are five sweet symphonies,
Cecily, Gertrude, Magdalen,
    Margaret and Rosalys."

Dante Gabriel Rossetti,
"The Blessed Damozel" (1847)

O daughters of dreams and of stories
    That life is not wearied of yet,
Faustine, Fragoletta, Dolores,
    Félise and Yolande and Juliette,
Shall I find you not still, shall I miss you,
    When sleep, that is true or that seems,
Comes back to me hopeless to kiss you,
    O daughters of dreams?

Algernon Charles Swinburne,
"Dedication" (1865)

The members are usually of different nationalities, and business is conducted either in the tongue each one knows best, or in what we call "French." Our "French" is the most remarkable language, except perhaps pidgin English, in the world. It should be spoken with a strong accent of your own to show your independence, and is a literal, or as near literal as one can manage, translation into French of the words of your own language in the order they usually occur. If you don't know the French for any word, you can either say it in your own tongue rather loud (to help the benighted foreigner to understand), or you can use any French word of a somewhat similar sound, if not meaning; or again you can simply gallicise the word itself by giving it what is here believed to be a French pronunciation, thus enriching that restricted language with a new word.

Lord Edward Cecil,
The Leisure of an Egyptian Official (1921)

Cecil's sketch of daily routine in Cairo is drawn from the eighteen years he spent attached to the Civil Service in Egypt before and after the First World War.

I once heard a missionary describe the extraordinary difficulty he had found in translating the Bible into Eskimo. It was useless to talk of corn or wine to a people who did not know what they meant, so he had to use equivalents within their powers of comprehension. Thus in the Eskimo version of the Scriptures the miracle of Cana of Galilee is described as turning the water into *blubber;* the 8th verse of the 5th chapter of the First Epistle of St. Peter ran: "Your adversary the devil, as a roaring polar bear walketh about, seeking whom he may devour." In the same way, "A land flowing with milk and honey" became "A land flowing with whale's blubber," and throughout the New Testament the words "Lamb of God" had to be translated "Little Seal of God . . ." The missionary added that his converts had the lowest possible estimate of Jonah for not having utilized his exceptional opportunities for killing and eating the whale.

Lord Frederic Hamilton,
The Days Before Yesterday (1930)

Hamilton's three volumes of diplomatic reminiscences also included The Vanished Pomps of Yesterday *and* Here, There and Everywhere.

A parody on Keats, first published in Franklin P. Adams' column in the New York Herald Tribune:

ON FIRST LOOKING INTO ROGET'S THESAURUS

"Much have I travell'd in the realms of gold—"

Much have I toured in xanthic zemindary,
And sundry tricksy scheses and garths perstringed
A mort of occidental aits I have befringed
That scalds *ro πρεπον* to Helios regrate in fee.
Da capo of unit discous range *on dit*
Which achroamatic Webster hegemoniously kinged:
But ne'er respired I its diaphaneity syringed
Till Roget quoth ophonic and chalybeate to me:
Betimes thole I as some empyrean vedette
When neoteric asteroids trudgeon and we see;
Or like athletic Cortez ophthalmic as aigrette
Ogled the Pacific and every devotee
Scrutinized reciprocally in corybantic bet—
Pauciloquious on a vertex in C. Z.

Dean Chamberlin (20th century American)

The Seven Sacraments are now all in my possession & as I mentioned to you in my letter of Aug. 24 in much better preservation than I had imagined, their apparent huskiness principally proceeding from the quantity of white of egg that was upon them . . .

James Byres

Byres was not, as one might suppose, conducting a delicate religious duty. He was an agent in Rome entrusted with buying some paintings by Poussin for a member of the British aristocracy. The source is Pryings Among Private Papers *(1905) by Thomas Longueville.*

An anonymous Southern slave captured the notes of liberty and happiness in the song of the Bobolink, a bird which abounded on rice plantations. His onomatopoetic rendition was quoted in Simeon Pease Cheney's Wood Notes Wild, Notations of Bird Music *(1892):*

Liberty, Liberty
Berry nice to be free!
Bob-o-link where he please,
Fly in de apple-trees;
Oh 'tis de freedom note
Guggle sweet in him troat.
Jink-a-link, jink-a-link,
Winky wink, winky wink,
Only tink, only tink
How happy, Bob-o-link!
Sweet! Sweet!

Pre-1855

The American painter James Abbott McNeill Whistler observes a rebellion in Chile with characteristic flourish, and in so doing helps us to understand the meaning of decadence:

5 March 1898   Volterra

In the evening we discussed the meaning of the word "decadent," Logan [Pearsall Smith, the writer's brother, see page 15] contending, quite rightly, I think, that it means a person who takes hold of important things by the handle of personal sensations, like Whistler, who, commanding a gun-boat in S. America during a rebellion, decided to join the party that had the best view of Valparaiso as the ships were manoeuvring, or a man who becomes a Catholic because he likes the smell of incense or the look of vestments.

Mary Berenson—A Self Portrait from Her Letters and Diaries (1983)

The Penobscot Indians of eastern Maine were early practitioners of nonsense lyrics. They believed song syllables to have magic power as, for example, in quieting the forces causing rough water and spurring canoe men forward. With this chant of quite meaningless syllables, recorded by Frank G. Speck in Penobscot Man *(1940), Indian singers tempered their voices to follow the pitching of the canoes as they mounted the waves:*

kwe há yu we, há yui we hí,
kwe hó yu we, hó yu we

The Penobscot tradition also appears to have had a rich vein of humor. A woman's song (again collected by Speck) , still current in this century and thought to be perfectly proper, translates as, "Where you come from it must be quite hot / Because your testicles are hanging so low."

Mrs. General informs her charge, Amy Dorrit, that fathers ought to be called "Papa":

"Father" is rather vulgar, my dear. The word "papa," besides, gives a pretty form to the lips. Papa, potatoes, poultry, prunes and prism, are all very good words for the lips; especially prunes and prism. You will find it serviceable in the formation of a demeanor, if you sometimes say to yourself in company,—on entering a room, for instance—Papa, potatoes, poultry, prunes and prism, prunes and prism.

Charles Dickens,
Little Dorrit (1857)

In his posthumously published The Epigram in the English Renaissance *(1947), Hoyt Hopewell Hudson chooses for an example of* carmen correlativum—*a construction in which all of the words have reference to each other respectively and match in an exact order—this specimen from the late sixteenth century in the* Harleian Miscellany, *translated in the manuscript by Saintlowe Knyvestonne:*

Pastor, arator, eques, paui, colui, superaui,
capras, rus, hostes, fonde, ligone, manu.

I sheppard	I plowman	I horseman light
Have fedd	have plowed	have put to flight
My goates	my grownde	my foes in feild
Wth bowes	wth plowes	with speare & sheild.

A hearde	a swaine	a noble knight
I fed	I tild	I did subdue
My goates	my growndes	my foes by flighte
Wth bowes	with plowes	these hands then slue.

31

Although the Bonjour family is still flourishing in Vevey, Switzerland, on the shores of Lake Geneva, only one of their grave markers was in evidence. when I visited the Cimitière Saint Martin in January 1988. That of a nineteenth century relative is no longer in view. But his epitaph fulfilled the literary obligations of the family:

LOUIS BONJOUR

1841-1896

AU REVOIR

Eponymous names:

The Magruder Principle: Telling the enemy what he already wants to believe; named after U.S. Colonel (later General) John T. Magruder by Colonel (later General) William Baumer, the U.S. representative to the London Controlling Section (LCS) in 1942-1943. The LCS was a secret bureau established by Prime Minister Winston Churchill within his personal headquarters to deceive Germany about Allied operations.

Mulligan: A second drive from the first tee, granted by some friendly amateur golfers to each other without loss of a stroke if the first drive is a bad shot; said to be named after a David Mulligan of the St. Lambert Country Club in Montreal in the 1920's. The extra shot, according to legend, was to compensate for any shakiness from driving his regular foursome to the golf club over a bumpy road.

Munro: A term referring to any Scottish peak over 3,000 feet, of which there are 277 in all; named after an engaging Victorian eccentric, Sir Hugh Munro (1856-1919), who set himself the task of climbing them but died when he was two peaks short of his goal. Munro published his *Table of Heights Over 3,000 Feet* in 1891.

In 1826 Thomas Bowdler published his revision of Edward Gibbon's
History of the Decline and Fall of the Roman Empire *for the use of
families and young persons, pledging to bury in oblivion all passages
of an irreligious or immoral tendency. He bowdlerized whole sections
offensive to church history but left untouched many of the best sections
on the vices of the Roman emperors. Here he edits one of Gibbon's
most famous sentences, on the third Gordian, who became Emperor in
238 A. D., but lets stand another on the death of the Empress Fausta in
326. A. D. The latter presumably conveys a moral to families and
young persons:*

	Gibbon	Bowdler
1.	Twenty-two thousand acknowledged concubines, and a library of sixty-two thousand volumes, attested the variety of his inclinations; and from the productions he left behind him, it appears the former as well as the latter were designed for use rather than for ostentation.	A library of sixty-two thousand volumes attested the variety of his studies; and from the productions he left behind him, it appears that his books were designed for use rather than for ostentation.

2. . . . nor was it long before a real or pretended discovery
    was made, that Fausta herself entertained a criminal
    connexion with a slave belonging to the Imperial stables.
    Her condemnation and punishment were the instant con-
    sequences of the charge; and the adultress was suffocated
    by the steam of a bath, which for that purpose had been
    heated to an extraordinary degree.

An exotic catalogue poem:

BILLS OF LADING

1650: *the Honourable East India Company to all Master Mariners:*
"We look that our vessels, ere launched on the seas
From Ind to Mozambique, be loaden with these:"

Sanguis draconis:
Fruges citronis:
Tramboon and cinnamon:
Myrrh and myrabalon:
Tamarind: olibanum:
Civet and cardamum:
Seed-lac and shellac:
Mastick and styrac:
Pepper and pepperdust:
Cloves garbled, ungarbled:
Bloodstones deep-marbled:
Attar and bela-scent:
Orris-root: orpiment:
Nutmegs and rubies:
Ginghams and sallampores:
Adatas and nassapores:
Newries and cocatores:
Percalloes and kastapores:
Gurrahs and balasores:
Calamdanes and scrutores:
Derribauds and kerebauds:
Byrampauts and durguzees:
Indigo and niccanees:

Turmeric and cavanees:
Grogerans and cuttanees:
Spikenard and dungarees:
Brawles: oringall bettelees:
Oppoponax and scamony:
Chequeens and toqueens:
Terrindans and nainsooks:
Doreas and tabbenees:
Taramandees: elatchees:
Sovaguzzees: pautkees:
Mercolees: egbarrees:
Morees and tapseils:
Damask and longees:
Benzoin and bezoar:
Red earth and redwood:
Dutties and rhanders:
Dihlee stuffs and khanders:
Birdseyes and deryeyes:
Diapers and dimitties:
Amber and ambergris:
Mullmulls and methelage:
Hornes of rhenosseries:
Chaubletts and romaulees:
Soosees: wax of bees:
Harital and patanees:
Tuttenagg and jellolsyes:
Chillies and baftas:
Benjamins and petambers:
Tanjebs and jemewars:
Vermilion and aloes
Both lignine and socatrine:
Sayes cantan and salloes:
Pillongs and lingloes:
Camphor and sannoes:

Safflower and rangoes:
Pumelos and mangoes:
Quicksilver and cossaes:
Hummums and chucklaes:
Duppetin catchaes:
And prinked perpentuanoes:
Allejars and pulfetoes:
Musk and salpicadoes:
Pearls and pintadoes:
Red cloths of China:
With taffaties of Persia:
And grezio corall
(Large-branched, well packt,
And free from dust and scruffe):
Buckshaws and wormseed:
Tincal and cowries:
Diamonds and cassia and elephants' teeth.

Edward Thompson
100 Poems (1944)

In addition to his poetry, Edward Thompson (1886-1946), who was long associated with India, wrote biography, novels and historical works.

Jung emphasized the importance of "meaningful coincidences," things which Arthur Koestler was later to call "puns of destiny."

Lyall Watson,
The Dreams of Dragons (1987)

COINCIDENCE

Coincidence
is bliss
numerical,
a tryst
of odds
or incidence
of sin
in God's
sabbatical
math'matical.

George Herrick,
11 January 1988

III. Idiosyncracies

Of Persians, in the sixth century B. C.:

It is also their general practice to deliberate upon affairs of weight when they are drunk; and then on the morrow, when they are sober, the decision to which they came the night before is put before them by the master of the house in which it was made; and if it is then approved of, they act on it; if not, they set it aside. Sometimes, however, they are sober at their first deliberation, but in this case they always reconsider the matter under the influence of wine.

Herodotus,
The Persian Wars, Book I, Chapter133

Two passages from the fourteenth-century traveller Ibn Batuta:

In China:

> He sent his son with us to the canal, where we went on board a ship resembling a fire-ship, and the amir's son went on another along with musicians and singers. They sang in Chinese, Arabic, and Persian. The amir's son was a great admirer of Persian melody, and when they sang a certain Persian poem he commanded them to repeat it over and over again, until I learned it from them by heart. It has a pleasant lilt, and goes like this:

> Ta dil bimihnat dadim
> dat bahr-i fikr uftadim
> Chun dar namaz istadim
> qavi bimihrab andarim.

> On this canal there was assembled a large crowd in ships with brightly-colored sails and silk awnings, and their ships too were admirably painted. They began a mimic battle and bombarded each other with oranges and lemons.

And in India:

> The space between the pavilions is carpeted with silk cloths, on which the sultan's horse treads. The walls of the street along which he passes from the gate of the city to the gate of the palace are hung with silk cloths. In front of him march footmen from his own slaves, several thousand in number, and behind come the mob and the soldiers. On one of his entries into the capital I saw three or four small catapults placed on elephants throwing gold and silver coins amongst the people from the moment when he entered the city until he reached the palace.

Abu-Abdallah Muhammad, called Ibn-Batuta,
Travels in Asia and Africa, 1325-1354,
H. A. R. Gibb, Tr.

Queen Elizabeth I writes rather severely to Heaton, the Bishop of Ely:

Proud Prelate,

I understand you are backward in complying with your agreement; but I would have you to know, that I, who made you what you are, can unmake you; and, if you do not forthwith fulfil your engagement, by ___ I will immediately unfrock you. Your's, as you demean yourself,

ELIZABETH

As a result of the letter, Heaton resolved his disagreement with the Queen.

June 18/1629/Thursday   Wind full W: and contrary to us. This day a notorious wicked fellow that was given to swearing and boasting of his formedness, bragged that hee had got a wench with child before hee came this voyage, and mocked at our daies of fast, railing and jesting agt puritans, this fellow fell sicke of the pockes and dyed. Wee sounded and found 38 fathm, and stayed for a little to take some codfish and feasted ourselves merily.

Francis Higginson,
"New England's Plantation"

The first form of writing distinctive of New England was the passage journal, which arose from the conversion of exploratory journals, or itineraria, into a variety of providential memorial devoted to representing the spiritual significance of a colonist's transatlantic passage. David Shields explores this literary landscape in ""A History of Personal Diary Writing in New England, 1620-1745," an unpublished University of Chicago doctoral dissertation (1982). Higginson, a dissenting minister from Leicester, sailed to the Massachusetts Bay Company's advance post at Salem in May 1629 and there established a church with a small group, including his friend Henry Herrick, also from Leicester. In describing New England, Higginson was to write, "a sup of New England's aire is better than a whole draught of Old England's ale."

Just eighteen years later, a few miles away from Salem, in Ipswich:

To speak moderately, I truly confess it is beyond the ken of my understanding to conceive how those women should have any true grace, or virtue, that have so little wit, as to disfigure themselves with such exotic garbs, as not only dismantles their native lovely lustre, but transclouts them into gant bar-geese, ill-shapen-shotten shell-fish, Egyptian hieroglyphics, or at the best into French flurts of the pastery, which a proper English woman should scorn with her heels. It is no marvel they wear drails on the hinder part of their heads, having nothing as it seems in the forepart, but a few squirrels' brains to help them frisk from one ill-favored fashion to another . . .

I can make myself sick at any time, with comparing the dazzling splendor wherewith our gentlewomen were embellished in some former habits, with the gut-foundered goosedom, wherewith they are now surcingled and debauched. We have about five or six of them in our colony: if I see any of them accidentally, I cannot cleanse my fancy of them for a month after. I have been a solitary widower almost twelve years, purposed lately to make a step over to my native country for a yoke-fellow: but when I consider how women there have tripe-wifed themselves with their cladments, I have no heart to the voyage, lest their nauseous shapes and the sea, should work too sorely upon my stomach. I speak sadly; methinks it should break the hearts of English men, to see so many goodly English women imprisoned in French cages, peering out of their hood holes for some men of mercy to help them with a little wit, and nobody relieves them.

Nathaniel Ward,
The Simple Cobbler of Agawam in America (1647)

John Aubrey (1626-1697) portrays Mary Herbert, Countess of Pembroke:

She was a beautifull Ladie and had an excellent witt, and had the best breeding that that age could afford. She had a pritty sharpe-ovall face. Her haire was of a reddish yellowe.

She was very salacious, and she had a Contrivance that in the spring of the yeare when the stallions were to leape the mares, they were to be brought before such a part of the house where she had a vidette to looke on them and please hereselfe with their Sport; and then shee would act the like sport herselfe with *her* stallions. One of her great gallants was crooke backt't Cecill, earl of Salisbury.

Brief Lives

The dean of American diarists has an awkward moment:

March, 27th [1706]   I walk in the Meetinghouse.   Set out homeward, lodg'd at Cushing's.   Note.   I pray'd not with my Servant, being weary.   Seeing no Chamber-pot call'd for one;   A little before day I us'd it in the Bed, and the bottom came out, and all the water run upon me.   I was amaz'd, not knowing the bottom was out till I felt it in the Bed.   The Trouble and Disgrace of it did afflict me.   As soon as it was Light, I calld up my man and he made a fire and warm'd me a clean Shirt and I put it on, and was comfortable. How unexpectedly a man may be expos'd!   There's no security but in God, who is to be sought by Prayer.

Samuel Sewall,
Diary

Louis XIV's sister-in-law, known officially as Madame and privately as Liselotte, writes to her aunt, the Duchess of Hanover, in her engaging manner. Liselotte's unwillingness to accept all of the conventions of Versailles, and her sense of fun, give her letters a special flavor:

Versailles 19 January 1710   You probably know that the Duc de Bourgogne is so pious that he won't look at anyone but his wife. To tease him, she once asked Mme de la Vrillière to get into bed in her place. The Duchesse pretended to be very tired that evening. He was delighted to find her ready for bed first for once, and undressed as quickly as possible. When he came into the room he asked, "Where is madame?", she answered "Here" from behind the curtain, and he flung off his dressing-gown and leapt into bed. As soon as he was under the bedclothes she came out and made a great pretence of being angry. "You claim to be devout," she said, "yet here you are, between the sheets with one of the prettiest ladies in the kingdom!" He asked her what she was talking about. She told him to take a look at the person who was lying beside him, and he fell into a fury. He took his "bedwarmer" by the shoulders and threw her out of bed, without giving her time to catch her breath or put on her slippers. Then he set about her with his own slippers. She escaped barefoot, he couldn't catch her, but called her every sort of name—effrontée and vilaine were the least of them. They tried to calm him, but they were laughing so much that they could hardly speak. In the end he cooled down.

A few days ago, when the Maréchale de Coeuvres tried to kiss him he defended himself with all his might. When he saw he was losing the struggle he stuck a pin into her head so hard that she has had to keep to her bed ever since. Even Joseph himself didn't go to such lengths—he only ran away and left his coat behind, but neither did he flail about him nor jab pins in. Such chastity as this has not been seen before.

Elizabeth Charlotte, Princess Palatine and Duchess of Orleans,
Letters

48

I rose about 8 o'clock, having first rogered my wife. I read a little in my commonplace book. I said my prayers and drank chocolate for breakfast.

William Byrd,
The Secret Diary of William Byrd of Westover

Planter, colonial official and author, William Byrd (1674-1744) was the second generation of the Byrd family of Virginia.

State funerals seem to bring out the best in participants and observers.
This is a scene from the funeral of George II:

This grave scene was fully contrasted by the burlesque Duke of Newcastle. He fell into a fit of crying the moment he came into the chapel, and flung himself back in a stall, the Archbishop hovering over him with a smelling-bottle—but in two minutes his curiosity got the better of his hypocrisy, and he ran about the chapel with his glass to spy who was or was not there, spying with one hand, and mopping his eyes with t'other. Then returned the fear of catching cold, and the Duke of Cumberland, who was sinking with heat, felt himself weighed down, and turning around, found it was the Duke of Newcastle standing upon his train to avoid the chill of marble.

Horace Walpole, to George Montagu, 13 November 1760,
Letters

For whatever reason, Boswell failed to record, during his tour through Scotland with Johnson in 1773, an amusing scene which took place over dinner on 29 August at an inn in Aberdeen. Robert Carruthers, editor of Boswell's Journal of a Tour to the Hebrides with Samuel Johnson, LL.D.*, captured the details from the Reverend Alexander Grant, who was present:*

Mr. Grant used to relate that on this occasion Johnson was in high spirits. In the course of conversation he mentioned that Mr. Banks (afterwards Sir Joseph) had, in his travels in New South Wales, discovered an extraordinary animal called the kangaroo. The appearance, conformation, and habits of this quadruped were of the most singular kind; and in order to render his description more vivid and graphic, Johnson rose from his chair and volunteered an imitation of the animal. The company stared; and Mr. Grant said nothing could be more ludicrous than the appearance of a tall, heavy, grave-looking man, like Dr. Johnson, standing up to mimic the shape and motions of a kangaroo. He stood erect, put out his hands like feelers, and, gathering up the tails of his huge brown coat so as to resemble the pouch of an animal, made two or three vigorous bounds across the room!

Goethe discusses religion with a papal military officer on the road to Perugia:

Perugia, October 25 [1786]

He had obviously noticed that I was a Protestant, so, after some beating about the bush, he asked if I would mind answering a few questions, because he had heard so many odd things about Protestants and would like to obtain some first-hand information at last. "Are you really allowed," he said, "to have an affair with a pretty girl without being married to her? Do your priests permit you that?" I replied: "Our priests are sensible men who do not bother themselves about such minor matters; of course, if we asked their permission, they would not give it." "And you really don't have to ask them?" he cried. "Oh, you lucky people! And, since you don't go to confession, they won't hear about it." Whereupon he began abusing his priests and praising our blessed freedom. "But confession," he went on, "what about that? We are told that all people, even those who are not Christians, must confess their sins. Since they are impenitent and cannot do it in the proper way, they make confession to an old tree, which is certainly silly and wicked, but still a proof that they recognize the necessity for confession."

Johann Wolfgang von Goethe,
Italian Journey,
W. H. Auden and Elizabeth Mayer, Tr.

John Quincy Adams found that some Parisian ladies did not like to discuss economics. His diary records a dinner at the celebrated Madame de Staël's, where the company included General Lafayette, several other gentlemen, and one other lady:

Feb. 15 [1815]

There were seventeen persons at the table. The conversation was not very interesting—some conversation between the lady and Mr. Constant, who seemed to consider it as a principle to contradict her. At one time there were symptons of a conversation arising upon a subject of political economy, upon which she said, "J'interdis tout discours sur l'économie politique. Ah! je crains l'économie politique—comme le feu."

John Quincy Adams,
Diary

It is unfortunate that Squire Waterton is seen by some as merely a vintage English eccentric. For he was also a pioneer conservationist, taxidermist and birdwatcher, as well as an intrepid traveller. On various occasions, he scaled St. Peter's in Rome, investigated the use of curare, and rode on the back of a reluctant crocodile. Here he seizes the initiative from an agitated boa constrictor in the wilds of Guyana:

The snake instantly turned, and came on at me, with his head about a yard from the ground, as if to ask me, what business I had to take liberties with his tail. I let him come, hissing and open-mouthed, within two feet of my face, and then, with all the force I was master of, I drove my fist, shielded by my hat, full in his jaws. He was stunned and confounded by the blow, and ere he could recover himself, I had seized his throat with both hands, in such a position that he could not bite me; I then allowed him to coil himself around my body, and marched off with him as my lawful prize. He pressed me hard, but not alarmingly so.

Charles Waterton,
Wanderings in South America (1825)

"Péronne la Pucelle, Sir?" "Aye, Péronne la Pucelle—it had never been taken before (smiling); but the Duke of Marlborough without Cambray and without Péronne could not and ought not to have advanced. Besides, countries were then much less thickly peopled or provided with supplies than they are now; armies can now move with much greater ease. But even now—what was it but the possession of the Spanish fortresses that obliged me to wait so long upon their frontier? I was obliged to wait till Pamplona and St. Sebastian had fallen—I could not stir before.

"Those fortresses were got by the French in the most infamous manner. Pamplona they took by the snow—the garrison were playing at snowballs, and the French advanced under pretence of joining in their sport. Barcelona the same sort of way."

Lord Stanhope,
Notes of Conversations with the Duke of Wellington, 1831-1851

Wellington was referring to the capture of Pamplona by the French from the Spanish in 1807.

In Three Years in the Sixth Corps *(1866), George T. Stevens, a surgeon with the 77th Regiment of Volunteers from Saratoga Springs, New York, has a colorful description of a regimental snowball fight between the Second Vermont and the Twenty-Sixth New Jersey. To break the monotony of camp life, General Joseph Hooker had instituted a number of diversions for the troops during his reorganization of the Army of the Potomac in early 1863. Because of his own diversions, Washington's army of prostitutes became known as "Hooker's girls," or "hookers."*

The pastor of the Second Presbyterian Church in Albany, New York, warns his daughter about reading novels. The first edition of 1821 was revised and enlarged. There were at least two British editions of this book:

But there is no species of reading to which young females are usually more inclined, or from which they are so much in danger, as that of novels. I will not say that there are no works of this kind which indicate a tone of correct moral feeling, and which are of unexceptionable moral tendency. Nor will I take it upon me to pass severe judgment upon many persons of great excellence, who have indulged in this kind of reading, on the ground that it furnishes many important lessons in respect to the operations of the human heart. But I must say, after an attentive consideration of this subject, and withal, after having once held a somewhat different opinion, that I do not wish you ever to read a novel. For admit that the novels of Richardson, and some of the modern novels of Scott, and a few others, abound with critical views of human nature, and contain many specimens of eloquent writing; and in their direct moral influence may be regarded as harmless—I cannot doubt that the time which you would occupy in reading them might be employed to better purpose in studying the actual realities of life, as they are exhibited by the biographer or the historian: and moreover, there is danger, if you begin to read works of fiction, with an intention to read but few, and to confine yourself to the better class, that your relish for these productions will increase, till you can scarcely feel at home unless the pages of a novel are spread out before you; and what is still more to be dreaded, that you will read indiscriminately, the most corrupt as well as the least exceptionable. You may rest assured that a character, formed under the influence of novel reading, is miserably fitted for any of the purposes of practical life.

William B. Sprague,
Letters on Practical Subjects to a Daughter (1834)

*The same hostility toward novels appears to have been prevalent in
America almost a generation later. There does not seem to have been
an edition of this book in Britain, where the novel was flourishing:*

If, instead of this kind of reading, mere fiction be resorted to, a puny
intellectual growth will be the consequence, and, instead of there
being the soundness of true mental force and discrimination, there
will be only the weakness of a trifling sentimentality.

T. S. Arthur,
Advice to Young Men on Their Duties and Conduct in Life (1860)

A good cigar, from a Cuba to a Principe, should burn with a clear steady glow, and leave a firm grey pellet of ashes as it consumes, which forms, by the way, the finest dentifrice that can be used.

E. L. Blanchard,
The Cigar and Smoker's Companion (1845)

This belongs to a category of things that are both cause and cure. White wine, for example, will sometimes act as an antidote for red wine stains.

For his mistress, Flaubert reflects on his encounters with the courtesan
Kuchuk Hanem, in Cairo in 1850:

. . . You tell me that Kuchuk's bedbugs degrade her in your eyes; for
me they were the most enchanting touch of all. Their nauseating
odor mingled with the scent of her skin, which was dripping with
sandalwood oil. I want a bitter undertaste in everything—always a
jeer in the midst of our triumphs, desolation in the very midst of
enthusiasm.

Gustave Flaubert,
Letter to Louise Colet, 27 March 1853,
Francis Steegmuller, Tr.

During the Civil War it was considered dishonorable to withdraw from the battlefield. Near Smithfield, Virginia, on 28 August 1864, Lieutenant Joseph S. Hoyer of the Nineteenth New York Cavalry had the ultimate excuse:

In one of these skirmishes my regiment, the 1st U.S. Cavalry, especially distinguished itself. Gen. Merritt says "by a splendid charge against double its numbers of the enemy, repelling his charge and driving his column back in confusion. In this charge Lieut. Hoyer of the 1st, a gallant and promising young officer, fell mortally wounded while leading his squadron." The regiment to which 1st Cavalry was opposed in this encounter was known as the Jeff Davis Legion, and was regarded by the enemy as one of their best cavalry regiments. Hoyer's was a singular case. He was shot at very close quarters with a pistol ball, but said nothing to anyone and retained command of his squadron until the enemy were driven off; then he rode up to Capt. Sweitzer and saluting him, asked permission to leave the column. "What for, Mr. Hoyer?" said Sweitzer, naturally a good deal surprised at the request under the circumstances. "Because I am mortally wounded, sir," answered poor Hoyer, without changing countenance. He was taken charge of in a moment and everything possible done for him, but his case was perfectly hopeless as he knew from the first, and he died in a few hours.

Fighting Rebels and Redskins,
Experiences in Army Life of Colonel George Sanford, 1861-1892

Victorian hygiene:

Sunday, Christmas Day [1870]

As I lay awake praying in the early morning I thought I heard a
sound of distant bells. It was an intense frost. I sat down in my
bath upon a sheet of thick ice which broke in the middle into large
pieces whilst sharp points and jagged edges stuck all around the sides
of the tub like chevaux de frise, not particularly comforting to the
naked thighs and loins, for the keen ice cut like broken glass. The
ice water stung and scorched like fire. I had to collect the floating
pieces of ice and pile them on a chair before I could use the sponge
and then I had to thaw the sponge in my hands for it was a mass of
ice. The morning was most brilliant. Walked to the Sunday School
with Gibbins and the road sparkled with millions of rainbows, the
seven colours gleaming in every glittering point of hoar frost. The
Church was very cold in spite of two roaring fires.

Rev. Francis Kilvert,
Diary

It is because authors so enjoy them that footnotes are a rich source of amusement. Here is a bit of learning that could not be squeezed into the text:

In some very warm climates the desires of the women are so imperious and exacting that the men are obliged to wear girdles to protect them from the women.

John Davenport,
Curiositates Eroticae Physiologiae
Or, Tabooed Subjects Freely Treated (1875)

Only someone with firsthand experience could have used the word "exacting."

A celebrated naturalist climbs a 100-foot Douglas spruce during a storm in the California mountains in December 1874 to get his ear "close to the Aeolian music of its topmost needles":

. . . never before did I enjoy so noble an exhilaration of motion. The slender tops fairly flapped and swished in the passionate torrent, bending and swirling backward and forward, round and round, tracing indescribable combinations of vertical and horizontal curves, while I clung with muscles firm braced, like a bobolink on a reed . . .

I kept my lofty perch for hours, frequently closing my eyes to enjoy the music by itself, or to feast quietly on the delicious fragrance that was streaming past. The fragrance of the woods was less marked than that produced during warm rain, when so many balsamic buds and leaves are steeped like tea; but, from the chafing of resiny branches against each other, and the incessant attrition of myriads of needles, the gale was spiced to a very tonic degree. And besides the fragrance from these local sources there were traces of scents brought from afar. For this wind came first from the sea, rubbing against its fresh, briny waves, then distilled through the redwoods, threading rich ferny gulches, and spreading itself in broad undulating currents over many a flower-enameled ridge of the coast mountains, then across the golden plains, up the purple foot-hills, and into these piny woods with the varied incense gathered by the way . . .

John Muir,
The Mountains of California (1894)

A Southern poet and planter looks back on his boyhood in Mississippi:

Without them it would probably never have occurred to me that to climb an aspen sapling in a gale is one of those ultimate experiences, like experiencing God or love, that you need never to try to remember because you can never forget. Aspens grow together in little woods of their own, straight, slender, and white. Even in still weather they twinkle and murmur, but in a high wind you must run out and plunge among them, spattered with sunlight, to the very center. Then select your tree and climb it high enough for it to begin to wobble with your weight. Rest your foot-weight lightly on the frail branches and do most of your clinging with your arms. Now let it lunge, and gulp the wind. It will be all over you, slapping your hair in your eyes, stinging your face with bits of bark and stick, tugging to break your hold, roaring in your open mouth like a monster sea-shell. The trees around you will thrash and seethe, their white undersides lashed about like surf, and sea-music racing through them. You will be beaten and bent and buffeted about and the din will be so terrific your throat will invent a song to add to the welter, pretty barbaric, full of yells and long calls. You will feel what it is to be the Lord God and ride a hurricane; you will know what it is to have leaves sprout from your toes and finger-tips, with satyrs and tigers and hounds in pursuit; you will never need again to drown under the crash of a maned wave in spume and splendor and thunder, with the white stallions of the sea around you, neighing and pawing.

William Alexander Percy,
Lanterns on the Levee—Recollections of a Planter's Son (1941)

64

Dancing in Ohio . . .

One of the things we did in those days was to take our visitors to the weekly dance at the Hospital for the Insane. The Ohio capital has many state institutions. Governor Alger danced with the patients. "I know now how to distinguish between the sane and the insane," he said to me, between waltzes; "the insane do not wear corsets."

Julia B. Foraker,
I Would Live It Again (1932)

The author was the widow of Joseph Benson Foraker (1846-1917), a conspicuous figure in Ohio Republican politics as Governor, then Senator, who was remembered for the phrase, "No rebel flags will be surrendered while I am Governor." Russell Alexander Alger (1836-1907) was Governor of, and later Senator from, Michigan and Secretary of War in McKinley's Cabinet.

And when they did come, our relations with them were strangely formal and mannered. We waltzed with them at the Balls and they were in our arms, but for the thoughts and words we exchanged with them it was still the age of the square-dance and the minuet. There were prescribed reticences, and distances to be kept; approaches and withdrawals were made to the beat of a traditional and accepted measure. Chaperones sat close at hand, veiling from us and our partners alike the experience in their eyes. Only at supper did the chaperones, but not the girls, admit to shared appetites.

L. E. Jones,
An Edwardian Youth (1956)

A Victorian Boyhood *(1955) and* Georgian Afternoon *(1958) complete the autobiographical trilogy of this British writer, and son of Balliol College, Oxford, who appears frequently, for example, in the pages of* The Lyttelton Hart-Davis Letters.

An anecdote about Queen Victoria:

One evening, sitting outside the Café de la Paix with Oscar Wilde, we were joined at our table by Caton Woodville, the war correspondent. He was something of a Münchhausen, and liked to boast of his exploits. He had recently been painting a picture for Queen Victoria—I forget what the subject was—in which the Queen herself was portrayed. When it was finished, he received a command to take it to Windsor. He described how Her Majesty entered the room, went up to the picture, examined it carefully in silence and then walked towards the door. As she opened the door she turned round and said coldly, "We are redder than that, Mr. Woodville," and swept out.

William Rothenstein,
Men and Memories (1931)

The sheer length of everything about A la Recherche du Temps Perdu *can blind us to Proust's mastery of the brief description. And the many veins of his irony make us forget that he can sometimes be witty:*

Next to her M. de Guermantes, superb and Olympian, was ponderously seated. One would have said that the notion, omnipresent in all his members, of his vast riches gave him a particular high density, as though they had been melted in a crucible into a single human ingot to form this man whose value was so immense. At the moment of my saying good-bye to him he rose politely from his seat, and I could feel the dead weight of thirty millions which his old-fashioned French breeding set in motion, raised, until it stood before me. I seemed to be looking at that statue of Olympian Zeus which Pheidias is said to have cast in solid gold. Such was the power that good breeding had over M. de Guermantes, over the body of M. de Guermantes at least, for it had not an equal mastery over the ducal mind. M. de Guermantes laughed at his own jokes, but did not unbend to other people's.

Marcel Proust,
Le Côté de Guermantes I (1920),
C. K. Scott Moncrieff, Tr.

In Lady Desborough at Taplow I was meeting a famous Edwardian beauty, wit and member of Souls. I had not realized the total self-confidence of a true *grande-dame* until I witnessed, through the library window, a little incident on the lawn outside. White-bearded Lord D'Abernon, ex-ambassador and once known as the handsomest man in England, was walking up and down on the grass arm in arm with Lady Desborough. Suddenly he tripped, fell flat on his face and brought down Lady Desborough with him. They both quietly righted themselves, linked arms again and continued their tottering stroll as if nothing had happened.

Elizabeth Longford,
The Pebbled Shore (1986)

British writer and illustrator Osbert Lancaster's description of one of his mother-in-law's tea parties on the Isle of Wight yields a splendid addition to parrot lore:

Too often the rare occasions when she did make a social effort and extended a conventional hospitality to her neighbours were, through no fault of hers, doomed to disaster. Once she braced herself to invite to tea a certain Colonel and Mrs. Savill, the most exalted and strait-laced of all the representatives of local society, and did her very best to create an unmistakeable atmosphere of gracious living. Exquisite in coffee-coloured lace she presided over tea on the lawn, the butler and parlour-maid hovered around with petits-fours and cucumber sandwiches, while all the house- party, for once properly attired, made polite conversation. Everything was going swimmingly and Mrs. Savill was just launched on a long account of last night's ball at the Garland Club when there came a voice from Heaven, "Fuck-off, you silly bitch!", and a gigantic orange and blue macaw planed gracefully down from the top of the Wellingtonia.

With an Eye to the Future (1967)

He [Lord Stodart of Leaston] told *The Times* that he had been chatting with them [the pelicans of St. James's Park] since 1959 when he became MP for Edinburgh West. He recalled rehearsing his maiden speech in Parliament on the pelicans to the accompaniment of the dawn chorus as he made his way through St. James's Park.

"Not a soul was looking and the pelicans seemed to be quite appreciative. Later I was told I was not the only one who did this although no one admitted it to each other."

Interestingly, that speech concerned the Mental Health Bill (Scotland) under the provisions of which the police were allowed to hold a person deemed to be exhibiting eccentric behaviour for 48 hours without informing relatives.

The Times (London),
18 December 1987

Prime Minister Churchill takes a briefing from his Private Secretary for a meeting with President Roosevelt on the postwar occupation of Germany:

September 12th, 1944

At the end of a Chiefs of Staff meeting, over which the P. M. presided, I heard him say to Portal that he might discuss with the President this evening the vexed "Zones of Occupation" question. Knowing he had not read the briefs on the subject and that there was no time for him to do so before dinner, I volunteered to read them aloud to him in his bath. This bizarre procedure was accepted, but the difficulties were accentuated by his inclination to submerge himself entirely from time to time and thus become deaf to certain passages.

John Colville,
The Fringes of Power—10 Downing Street Diaries (1985)

Chinese leader Deng Xiaoping plays bridge:

Deng, like many in Yan'an, had become fond of bridge. Some international bridge players rate him world class. Once he came into power, he played almost every day. He had for his partner Wan Li, Politburo member, vice-premier, onetime deputy mayor of Beijing, old friend and early victim of the Cultural Revolution. Sometimes, it was said, he played with General Yang Shangkum. Another player was Ding Guang-lu, vice-secretary general of the People's Congress. Katherine Wei, a championship bridge player in New York, has played with Deng and calls him a fine competitor. He told her that bridge "keeps my mind sharp." He plays to win, but not for money. The loser must crawl under a table. When Deng loses, his partners always say, "Oh, you don't have to do that." He invariably responds: "Yes, I will. It is the rule of the game." And he crawls under a table, a bit easier for him because of his diminutive stature.

Harrison Salisbury,
The Long March (1985)

73

IV. Le Mot Juste

It was the epoch of the *mot juste*. I craved for myself as well as for my pupils a greater mastery of exact terms, and we worked away (for I took each assignment with them) on the precise rendering of observed form, color, sound, and motion. I assured the class that when they could describe a goldfinch singing in its billowy flight they could write English!

Bliss Perry,
And Gladly Teach—Reminiscences (1935)

Perry was a professor of English Literature at Harvard College from 1906 to 1930.

Perhaps Perry had Keats in mind:

Sometimes goldfinches one by one will drop
From low hung branches; little space they stop;
But sip, and twitter, and their feathers sleek;
Then off at once, as in a wanton freak:
Or perhaps, to show their black and golden wings,
Pausing upon their yellow flutterings.

John Keats,
"I Stood Tip-Toe Upon a Little Hill" (1817)

It was after this fancy about *rouble* occurred to me that I read the account by Lucien Fabre of a word-problem posed by Valéry. The two men were watching a small stream of water escape from a sluice, as it picked its way along and disposed of tiny pebbles this way and that, as though of set purpose to clear a bed for itself in the sand. What single adjective, asked Valéry, would serve at once matter and spirit—would both picture the pebbly stream and convey its hesitant, deliberate mood?

Nous restâmes silencieux un moment.
—Et si, lui proposai-je, si nous disions: le ruisseau scrupuleux?
Il se redressa, ravi: —Bravo, dit-il. Scrupulus, petit caillou. Le mot existait donc! . . . Vous, vous l'avez trouvé.
Il me serra le bras, ajouta avec un demi-rire qui cachait mal une vraie émotion:
—Il l'a trouvé! Ah! on sait bien pourquoi on l'aime, ce Lucien!

The word *scrupuleux*, lucky also in absorbing the sound of water, might be said to have done treble duty.

G. R. Hamilton,
Guides and Marshals (1950)

Engineer, philosopher and novelist (Prix Goncourt, 1923), Lucien Fabre was a leading disciple of Paul Valéry, who described his friend as a Renaissance man.

Finally we talked about Flaubert, about his methods, his patience, his seven years spent on a single book of four hundred pages. "Imagine!" exclaimed Gautier. "The other day Flaubert said to me: 'It's finished. I have only ten more pages to write. But I have already got the ends of the sentences.' You see? He already had the music of the ends of the sentences which he hadn't yet begun . . . You know the poor fellow has one remorse that is poisoning his life. It's going to put him in the grave. You don't know what that remorse is. It's that in *Madame Bovary* he stuck two genitives one right on top of the other: *Une couronne de fleurs d'oranger.* It made him miserable; but there was not a thing he could do about it, try as he did."

Edmond and Jules de Goncourt,
Journal,
Lewis Galantière, Tr.

The books in Macaulay's library contained running commentaries and notes in immense profusion down their margins. His nephew, Sir George Otto Trevelyan, shared some of them with us in Marginal Notes of Lord Macaulay *(1907), a small volume which may be unique of its kind.*

He enjoyed and valued Cicero's Letters to a degree that he found difficult to express. The document which he most admired, in the whole collection of the correspondence, was Caesar's answer to Cicero's message of gratitude for the humanity which the conqueror had displayed towards those political adversaries who had fallen into his power at the surrender of Corfinium. It contained, (so Macaulay used to say,) the finest sentence ever written: "Meum factum probari abs te, triumpho, gaudeo. Neque illud me movet quod ii, qui a me dimissi sunt, discessisse dicuntur ut mihi rursus bellum inferrent; nihil enim malo quam et me mei similem esse, et illos sui." Opposite that sentence appear the words: "Noble Fellow!"

The translation given by Trevelyan for Caesar's phrase is:

I triumph and rejoice that my action should have obtained your approval. Nor am I disturbed when I hear it said that those, whom I have sent off alive and free, will again bear arms against me; for there is nothing which I so much covet as that I should be like myself and they like themselves.

In answer to the question as to which of all the lines he [Alfred Tennyson] had written he was proudest of, he said, "I think I am most glad to have written the line,

'The mellow ouzel fluted in the elm.'

I think I was the first to describe the ouzel (or blackbird)'s flute note."
"But," said I, "what about

'The moan of doves in immemorial elms,
And murmuring of innumerable bees.'?

"Well," he answered, "I am glad to have written those also."

Rev. H. D. Rawnsley,
Memories of the Tennysons (1900)

The Poet Laureate's line comes from "The Gardener's Daughter" (1833-1834):

To left and right,
The cuckoo told his name to all the hills;
The mellow ouzel fluted in the elm;
The redcap whistled; and the nightingale
Sang aloud, as tho' he were the bird of day.

This passage on the virtue of a certain negligence in style comes from an unpublished doctoral dissertation by John W. Howland, The Letter in Eighteenth Century French Literature, *University of California (1984):*

L'exactitude Grammaticale n'est pas absolument nécessaire dans le Stile Epistolaire: Pourvu que vous ne fassiez pas de faute contre la Langue, de petites négligences contre la Grammaire ne deplaîront pas, sur-tout si vous ne les commettez que pour vous exprimer plus vivement, plus délicatement, ou plus finement.

Eléazar de Mauvillon,
Traité Général du Stile avec un traité particulier du Stile Epistolaire (1756)

The Abbé Nicolas Charles Joseph Trublet (1697-1770) expressed a similar thought in Essais de morale et de littérature *(1735):*

Negligencies give a natural air to writing, by discharging it of an air of labor and stiffness; and it is in this sense that they are sometimes reckoned among the graces of style.

A curious figure in French literature, Trublet, who thought his use of the comma bordered on the sublime, earned Voltaire's ridicule as a compiler of other men's adages, but nevertheless gained a place in the Académie Française—after a long wait.

V. Unusual Letters and Inscriptions

The above queen [Nictoris] was also celebrated for another instance of ingenuity: she caused her tomb to be erected over one of the principal gates at the city, and so situated as to be obvious to universal inspection: it was thus inscribed — "If any of the sovereigns, my successors, shall be in extreme want of money, let him open my tomb and take what money he may think proper; if his necessity be not great, let him forbear; the experiment will perhaps be dangerous." The tomb remained without injury til the time and reign of Darius. He was equally offended at the gate's being rendered useless, and that the invitation thus held out to become affluent should have been so long neglected. The gate, it is to be observed, was of no use, from the general aversion to pass through a place over which a dead body was laid. Darius opened the tomb; but instead of finding riches, he saw only the dead body, with a label of this import: "If your avarice had not been equally base and insatiable, you would not have intruded upon the repose of the dead."

Herodotus,
The Persian Wars,
William Beloe, Tr.

In later life Cicero would take pride in having, during his visit to Syracuse in 75 B.C., rediscovered the grave marker of Archimedes (who had died in 212 B. C.) , with its graphic inscription of a globe and a cylinder. The equivalent date today (1988) for the same lapse of time would be only 1851. That Archimedes' grave site could be all but forgotten reminds us of the separateness of their two civilizations.

. . . ex eadem urbe humilem homunculum a puluere et radio excitabo, qui multis annis post fuit, Archimedem. cuius ego quaestor ignoratum ab Syracusanis, cum esse omnino negarent, saeptum undique et uestitum uepribus et dumetis indagaui sepulcrum. tenebam enim quosdam senariolos, quos in eius monumento esse inscriptos acceperam, qui declarabant in sumo sepulcro sphaeram esse positam cum cylindro.

Tusculan Disputations (45 B.C.),
Book 5, XXIII.64

From the same city of Syracuse I shall rouse the most modest of men from his measuring rod and the dust in which he drew—one who lived many years later, Archimedes. Archimedes, whose tomb I tracked down while a quaestor, hedged about on all sides, shrouded in brambles and thickets and unnoticed by the locals, since they denied its existence altogether. For I had in my possession a few verses which I learnt were inscribed on his memorial, revealing that a globe and a cylinder had been set on the very top of the tomb.

A. J. Norman, Tr.

Consideration for inconveniencing one's friends is the best reason for not forgetting an invitation, but the anguish of missing a good dinner is another, as Pliny the Younger reminded a friend:

To Septicius Clarus

How happened it, my friend, that you did not keep your engagement the other night to sup with me? Now take notice, the court is sitting, and you shall fully reimburse me the expense I was at to treat you; which, let me tell you, was no small sum. I had prepared, you must know, a lettuce apiece and three snails for each, with two eggs, barley-water, some sweet wine and snow (the snow most certainly I shall charge to your account before everything else, since it melts on the tray in serving)! Besides all these curious dishes, there were olives, beets, gourds, shallots, and a hundred other dainties equally sumptuous. You should likewise have been entertained either with an interlude, the rehearsal of a poem, or a piece of music, as you like best; or (such was my liberality) with all three. But the oysters, chitterlings, sea-urchins and Spanish dancers of a certain—I know not who, were it seems more to your taste. However, I shall have my revenge on you, depend upon it;—in what manner, shall at present be a secret. In good truth it was not kind thus to mortify your friend—I had almost said yourself;—and upon second thought I do say so; for how agreeably should we have spent the evening in laughing, trifling, and deep speculation! You may sup, I confess, at many places more splendidly; but you can be treated nowhere, believe me, with more unconstrained cheerfulness, simplicity and freedom. Only make the experiment: and if you do not ever afterwards prefer my table to any other, never favour me with your company again. Farewell.

Caius Plinius Caecilius Secundus (born 61 A. D.),
Letters

Encountering a violent storm on his return from America, Columbus despaired that the world would ever learn of his great discovery. This is an abstract of the Admiral's journal by his companion, Las Casas:

February 14, 1493

On this account, and that their Highnesses might be informed that our Lord had granted success to the enterprise in the discovery of the Indies, and might know that storms did not prevail in those quarters, (which was apparent from the plants and trees growing down to the very brink of the sea,) he devised a method of acquainting them with the circumstances of the voyage in case they should perish in the storm; this he performed by writing upon parchment an account of it, as full as possible, and earnestly entreating the finder to carry it to the King and Queen of Spain. The parchment was rolled up in a waxed cloth, and well tied; a large wooden cask being then produced, he placed it within, and threw it into the sea, none of the crew knowing what it was, but all taking it for some act of devotion.

Christopher Columbus,
Journal

To my office, and there all the morning. At noon, being invited, I to the Sun behind the Change to dinner to my Lord Bellasses— where a great deal of discourse with him—and some good. Among other at table, he told us a very handsome passage of the King's sending him his message about holding out the town of Newarke, of which he was then governor for the King. This message he sent in a Slugg-bullet, being writ in Cypher and wrapped up in lead and swallowed. So the messenger came to my Lord and told him he had a message from the King, but it was yet in his belly; so they did give him some physic, and out it came. This was a month before the King's flying to the Scotts; and therein he told him that at such a day, being the 3 or 6 of May, he should hear of his being come to the Scotts, being assured by the King of France that in coming to them, he should be used with all the Liberty, Honour and safety that could be desired. And at the just day he did come to the Scotts.

Samuel Pepys,
Diary

I was, after the fashion of men, in love with my name, and wrote it down everywhere, as young, uncultured people are wont to do. Once I had cut it very finely and exactly on the smooth bark of a lime tree of moderate age. The following autumn, when my affection to Annette was in its fullest bloom, I took the trouble to cut hers above it. Meanwhile I had towards the end of the winter, as a capricious lover, seized many opportunities of teasing her and causing her vexation; by chance in the spring I visited the same spot, and the sap, which was rising strongly in the trees, had welled out through the incisions which formed her name and which were not yet hardened over and moistened, with innocent tears of the tree, traces of my own which had already become hard. Thus to see her here weeping over me, who had so often called up her tears by my unkindness, filled me with confusion. In the remembrance of my injustice and her love, tears came into my eyes. I hastened to ask pardon from her doubly and trebly, and turned this incident into an idyll, which I could never read to myself without affection or, to others, without emotion.

Johann Wolfgang von Goethe,
Autobiography,
R. O. Moon, Tr.

Book dedications are another interesting little garden of delight. A. E. Housman left this as an inscription for his posthumously published More Poems *(1936):*

> They say my verse is sad: no wonder;
>   Its narrow measure spans
> Tears of eternity, and sorrow,
>   Not mine, but man's.
>
> This is for all ill-treated fellows
>   Unborn and unbegot,
> For them to read when they're in trouble
>   And I am not.

Thackeray's dedication of Pendennis *(1848) reflects an unusual debt:*

To
Dr. John Elliotson

My dear Doctor,—Thirteen months ago, when it seemed likely that this story had come to a close, a kind friend brought you to my bedside, whence, in all probability, I never should have risen but for your constant watchfulness and skill. I like to recall your great goodness and kindness (as well as many acts of others, showing quite a surprising friendship and sympathy) at that time, when kindness and friendship were most needed and welcome

And as you would take no other fee but thanks, let me record them here in behalf of me and mine, and subscribe myself,

Yours most sincerely and gratefully,
W. M. Thackeray.

And I like the inscription of the anonymous author of The Martyrdom of St. George of Cappadocia *(1614):*

To all the Nobles, Honourable and Worthy in Great Britaine bearing the name of George . . .

VI. Envoi

The maritime history of Massachusetts, then, as distinct from that of America, ends with the passing of the clipper. 'Twas a glorious ending! Never, in these United States, has the brain of man conceived, or the hand of man fashioned, so perfect a thing as the clipper ship. In her, the long-suppressed artistic impulse of a practical, hard-worked race burst into flower. *The Flying Cloud* was our Rheims, the *Sovereign of the Seas* our Parthenon, the *Lightning* our Amiens; but they were monuments carved from snow. For a brief moment of time they flashed their splendor around the world, then disappeared with the sudden completeness of the wild pigeon. One by one they sailed out of Boston, to return no more. A tragic or mysterious end was the final privilege of many, favored by the gods. Others, with lofty rig cut down to cautious dimensions, with glistening decks and top-sides scarred and neglected, limped about the seas under foreign flags, like faded beauties forced upon the street.

Samuel Eliot Morison,
The Maritime History of Massachusetts (1921)

The ending of Alphonse Daudet's Kings in Exile *(1879):*

... and when the Tuileries, their ashes gilded by a departing ray, rise up before her to recall the past, she gazes at them without emotion, without memory, as though she looked upon some ancient ruin of Assyria or of Egypt, the witness of manners and of morals and of peoples vanished; a grand old dead past—gone.

The closing sentence, occurring to Daudet one evening in front of the Tuileries, gave him the inspiration for his novel.

Going into that strange world of unending day was like stepping very quietly across the invisible border of the land of Faery that the Irish poets write of, that timeless world of Fionn and Saeve, or the world of Thomas the Rhymer. It was evening when we left Baker Lake, but an evening that would never flower into night, never grow any older. And so we had set out, released from fear, intoxicated with a new sense of freedom—out into that clear unbounded sea of day. We could go on and on and never reach the shores of night. The sun would set, darkness would gather in the bare coves, creep over the waste lands behind us, but never overtake us. The wave of night would draw itself together, would rise behind us and never break.

Anne Morrow Lindbergh,
North to the Orient (1935)

Anne Morrow Lindbergh describes the magic of the first flight into the land of the midnight sun. She and her husband were flying from Baker Lake toward Point Barrow on the Great Circle route to Japan and China in 1931.

Leisure with dignity is a commendable goal. A friend of mine kindly sent me this on my retirement from the State Department this year:

London, February 9, 1748 (O.S.)

Dear Boy: You will receive this letter, not from a Secretary of State but from a private man; for whom, at his time of life, quiet was as fit, and as necessary, as labor and activity are for you at your age, and for many years yet to come. I resigned the seals, last Saturday, to the King; who parted with me most graciously, and (I may add, for he said so himself) with regret. As I retire from hurry to quiet, and to enjoy, at my ease, the comforts of private and social life, you will easily imagine that I have no thoughts of opposition, or meddling with business. *Otium cum dignitate* is my object. The former I now enjoy; and I hope that my conduct and character entitle me to some share of the latter. In short, I am now happy: and I found that I could not be so in my former public situation.

Lord Chesterfield,
Letters

The relish of the Muse consists in rhyme:
One verse must meet another like a chime.
Our Saxon shortness hath peculiar grace
In choice of words fit for the ending-place,
Which leaves impression in the mind as well
As closing sounds of some delightful bell.

Sir John Beaumont (1583-1627),
Concerning the True Form of English Poetry

Index of Authors

Index of Subjects

GEORGE GARDNER HERRICK was born in 1938. He had a Boston upbringing and his family lived for many years in Paris. He was educated at Harvard and Balliol College, Oxford. A retired State Department officer, he most recently served for five years at the London Embassy. He and his three sons live in Washington, D.C., and look forward to summers on a family island in Maine. He likes B's: Boston and books, birdwatching and bridge, baseball and bonfires.

He is the author of another commonplace book, *Michelangelo's Snowman*, which was published by The Ipswich Press in 1985.

The decorative border on the title page is the work of the American illustrator Will Bradley, 1896. The borders on the chapter division pages are from sketches by the German designer Paul Bürck, 1906.